# START-UP
# SCIENCE

# SOUND AND HEARING

## Claire Llewellyn

## CHERRYTREE BOOKS

Distributed in the United States by
Cherrytree Books
1980 Lookout Drive
North Mankato, MN 56001

U.S. publication copyright © Cherrytree Books 2005
International copyright reserved in all countries. No part
of this book may be reproduced in any form without
written permission from the publisher.

Library of Congress Cataloging-in-Publication Data
applied for

First Edition
9 8 7 6 5 4 3 2 1

First published in 2004 by
Evans Brothers Limited
2A Portman Mansions
Chiltern Street
London W1U 6NR
Copyright © Evans Brothers Limited 2004

Conceived and produced by

White-Thomson Publishing Ltd.

Editor: Dereen Taylor
Consultants: Les Jones, Science Consultant, Manchester
Education Partnership; Norah Granger, former primary
school principal and senior lecturer in education,
University of Brighton.
Designer: Leishman Design

**Picture Acknowledgments:**
Chris Fairclough Colour Library 6 (bottom left);
8 (left and right); 9 (left); Corbis 6 (top left, bottom
right); 13 (bottom); 16 (main); 17 (right); Ecoscene 4
(right);
7 (bottom left); 18, 19; Eye Ubiquitous 9 (right).
All other photographs by Chris Fairclough.

Printed in China

**Acknowledgments:**
The publishers would like to thank staff and pupils at
Elm Grove Primary School, for their involvement in the
preparation of this book.

# Contents

# A Sound Walk

◀ Dad and Luca are walking to school. They hear a lot of sounds on the way.

▶ They hear birds singing in the trees.

◀ They hear a motorcycle roaring down the street.

hear  sounds  singing

▲ **They hear children** shouting **in the playground.**

**What do you hear on your way to school?**

roaring   shouting

# All Sorts of Sounds

There are many **different** kinds of sounds in the world.

◀ Some are **loud**, like the engines of a plane.

▲ Some are **soft**, like the wind in the leaves.

▲ Some are **high**, like a violin.

▲ Some are **low**, like a cello.

different  loud  soft  high  low

Look at the things in the pictures on this page. What kinds of sounds do they make?

**WARNING!**
Very loud noises can hurt our ears.

noises hurt

# Different Places, Different Sounds

Different places have their own special sounds.
What would you expect to hear in these places?

**Train station**

**Woods**

How do these sounds make you **feel**?
What would these places sound like at **night**?
What different sounds might you hear?

Construction site

Beach

**feel  night**

# Our Bodies Make Sounds

Our bodies make many different sounds.

We make sounds when we speak and sing.

We can make plenty of other sounds, too!

▼Can you make these sounds?

Whistle!        Clap!        Achoo!

speak   sing   breathing   quiet

Our bodies make sounds as they work. Can you hear yourself breathing?

▼ Some body sounds are very quiet. You need a stethoscope to hear someone's heart beating.

Pop!

stethoscope   beating

# We Hear With Our Ears

▶ We hear sounds with our ears. Hearing is one of our body's senses.

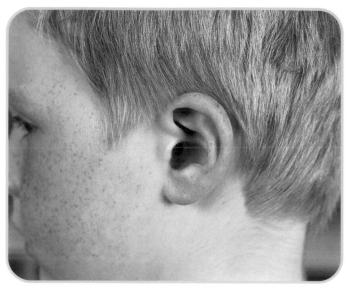

◀ Try closing your eyes and listening. What can you hear right now? What do the sounds - or the silence - tell you?

hearing   senses   listening   silence

Some people hear better than others.

▶ Cupping a hand around your ear helps you to hear more clearly.

People who are deaf cannot hear well. They may use a hearing aid and learn to read sign language.

deaf    hearing aid    sign language    **13**

# Near or Far?

Our ears tell us where a sound is coming from. They tell us whether the sound is near or far away. Things sound louder the nearer they are.

Kip gives Sam a hearing test. Kip takes one step back and whispers something softly. Then he moves back two more steps and does it again.

Each time, Sam tells him whether he can hear him or not.

Kip does the same with a whistle.

near  far away  louder  hearing test

Then Lily does the test with some bells.

The chart shows what Sam can hear.

| Strides | 1 | 5 | 10 |
|---|---|---|---|
| Whisper | ✔ | ✗ | ✗ |
| Bells | ✔ | ✔ | ✗ |
| Whistle | ✔ | ✔ | ✔ |

Which sound can Sam only hear close up?

Which sound can he hear from farthest away?

whispers   whistle   bells

# Hearing Keeps Us Safe

▲ Our hearing helps to keep us safe. We hear the "beep beep" sound at the pedestrian crossing. This tells us when it's safe to cross the road.

safe  beep beep  pedestrian crossing

▼ Drivers may hear a fire engine before they see it. Its siren tells them to clear the road so that it can get to the fire quickly.

▲ Animals also warn us with sound. A guard dog barks and growls to keep people away.

How does a cat show it is angry?

siren  warn  barks  growls

# Sound Words

There are many different **words to describe sounds.**
These are some of the words we use to describe
fireworks:

words        describe

Look at the sound words on this page.
Which ones best describe the sea in this picture?
Can you think of any others?

boom    clap    roar    rattle

tinkle    splash    whine    crash

Which of these pictures do you like best?
Maybe you could write a poem about it.

poem

# Sound Stories

▲ These pictures tell a **story**.

**wooden blocks**    **triangle**    **pitcher and cup**

▲ You could make **sound effects** for each picture, using the objects above.

**20**

**story**    **sound effects**

▼ **Put the sounds together and tell the story in sound. Then you could record your sound story.**

**crumpled paper**

**record**

# Further Information for

## New words listed in the text:

| | | | | | |
|---|---|---|---|---|---|
| barks | far away | hurt | pedestrian | shouting | sounds |
| beating | feel | listening | crossing | sign language | speak |
| beep beep | growls | loud | poem | silence | stethoscope |
| bells | hear | louder | quiet | sing | story |
| breathing | hearing | low | record | singing | warn |
| deaf | hearing aid | near | roaring | siren | whispers |
| describe | hearing test | night | safe | soft | whistle |
| different | high | noises | senses | sound effects | words |

## Possible Activities

### PAGES 4-5

Go on a sound walk around different parts of the school - both inside and outside. Ask children to keep quiet and to listen hard. Return to the classroom and talk about all the sounds they heard.

### PAGES 6-7

Allow the children to try out many kinds of musical instruments. How do they play them? What kind of sound is made? Which ones do they like/dislike? How can they make the instrument sound soft? How can they make it sound loud?

Sort the instruments into groups, according to how they are played. Draw or write lists of the different groups.

Make some homemade musical instruments, using rubber bands over a glass, sugar inside empty plastic pots; or some empty cardboard tubes. How would the children play these?

### PAGES 8-9

Ask children to predict the sounds they will hear in bed this evening, and make a list. The next day, ask them to remember what they actually heard. Compare the two different lists.

Find a big picture of a busy scene - e.g. a beach on a summer's day. Ask the children what sounds they would hear if they were there. Which ones would be loudest/softest?

### PAGES 10-11

Ask the children to touch their throat as they speak or sing. Can they feel a difference when they make a high sound and when they make a low, growly sound?

Ask the children to find different animal sounds on a CD-ROM or other resource.

### PAGES 12-13

Listen to a tape containing familiar sounds. Can the children identify them all?

# Parents and Teachers

Ask the children to cover their ears and walk around a room. Is it easy to walk around if you cannot hear? Make sure the environment is safe and ask them to shut their eyes as well.

Hide different things (e.g. a marble, a cork, a pencil, a paper clip, rice, cotton) inside a box. Can children identify the object by shaking the box?

## PAGES 14-15

Make a list or draw pictures of three sounds that can be heard from a long way away.

## PAGES 16-17

Discuss how animals (e.g. rabbits) rely on their hearing to keep them safe. Some animals (e.g. birds, monkeys) call to one another when danger is close.

Make a list of all the vehicles that have sirens, bells, musical sounds, or loudspeakers.

## PAGES 18-19

Collect pictures that could be the starting point for literacy work about sounds (e.g. a rocket launching, a grasshopper, a waterfall). Make a list of sounds to suit each picture. Can the children guess the picture from the list of words?

## PAGES 20-21

Ask the children to write a very simple story that could be told using sounds. Then ask them to collect objects that would make suitable sound effects. Record the sounds and perform the story.

## Further Information

### BOOKS FOR CHILDREN

Llewellyn, Claire. *The Best Ears in the World*.
Mankato, MN: Smart Apple Media, 2002.

Hewitt, Sally. *Hearing Sounds*.
New York: Children's Press, 1999.

Pluckrose, Henry. *Listening and Hearing*.
Chicago: Raintree, 1998.

Riley, Peter. *Sound*.
Milwaukee, MN: Gareth Stevens, 2002.

### BOOKS FOR ADULTS

Huns, Monica. *How to Sparkle at Science Investigations*.
Dunstable, UK: Brilliant Publications.

### WEB SITES

www.howstuffworks.com
www.niehs.nih.gov/kids/links.htm
www.sciencemaster.com

# Index